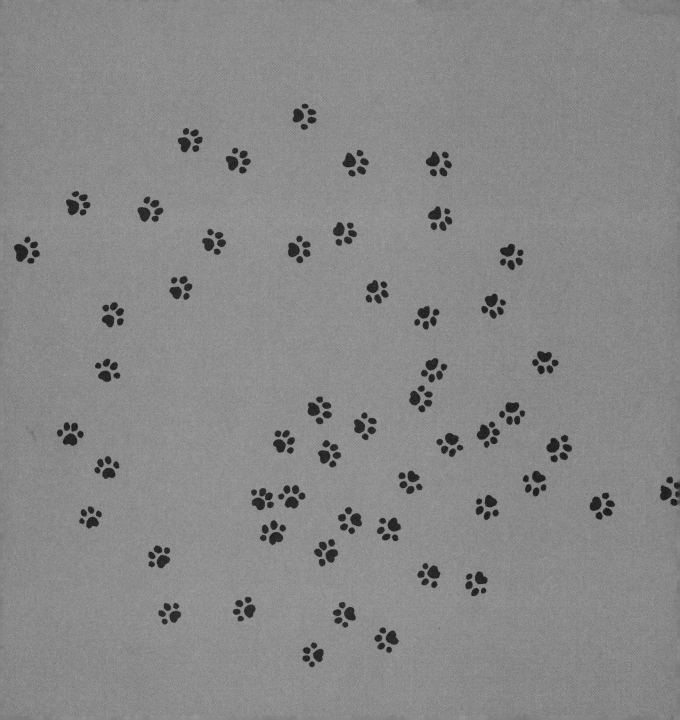

LET'S TALK ABOUT
FEELING
EMBARRASSED

by Joy Berry • Illustrated by Maggie Smith

SCHOLASTIC INC.

New York   Toronto   London   Auckland   Sydney
Mexico City   New Delhi   Hong Kong   Buenos Aires

ISBN 0-439-34164-7

10 9 8 7 6 5 4 3 2 1   02 03 04 05 06

Printed in the U.S.A.
First printing, July 2002

Hello, my name is Roma.

I live with Dillon.

Sometimes Dillon says or does something that makes him feel foolish.

Dillon feels embarrassed.

Sometimes, somebody else says or does
something that makes Dillon feel foolish.

Dillon feels embarrassed.

When you feel embarrassed, you might feel foolish.

You might also feel badly about yourself.

Your body might do strange things when you feel embarrassed.

You might blush.

You might suddenly feel very hot.

You might also feel like running away.

There are things you can do to avoid feeling embarrassed.

You can ignore the person who is embarrassing you.

Sometimes a person will continue to embarrass you even though you ignore them.

When this happens, ask them to leave you alone.

If someone keeps bothering you,
walk away.

Sometimes it's impossible to ignore someone who is embarrassing you.

Try not to be mean to that person.

Being mean will only make things worse.

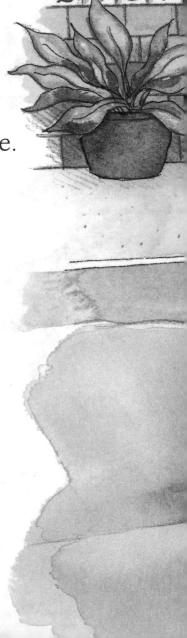

Sometimes it's impossible to avoid an embarrassing situation.

To make yourself feel better, talk to someone about how you feel.

Whenever you feel embarrassed, try to remember that nobody is perfect.

Everyone says or does embarrassing things once in a while.

Unfortunately, you can't change what's already happened.

So try not to waste time wishing you hadn't been embarrassed.

Thinking too much about an embarrassing situation will only make you feel worse.

It might even make the situation seem more embarrassing than it actually was.

Sometimes you might not want to be around the people who were with you when you were embarrassed.

Since you can't avoid them forever, remember that they have had embarrassing moments, too.

Whenever you feel embarrassed, remember that there is usually something funny about every embarrassing situation.

If you can laugh about the funny part, you will probably feel better!

Everyone feels embarrassed once in a while.

Feeling embarrassed is okay.

The important thing is to handle embarrassing situations in a positive way so that you feel better about them.

Let's talk about... **Joy Berry!**

As the inventor of self-help books for kids, Joy Berry has written over 250 books that teach children about taking responsibility for themselves and their actions. With sales of over 80 million copies, Joy's books have helped millions of parents and their kids.

Through interesting stories that kids can relate to, Joy Berry's Let's Talk About books explain how to handle even the toughest situations and emotions. Written in a clear, simple style and illustrated with bright, humorous pictures, the Let's Talk About books are fun, informative, and they really work!

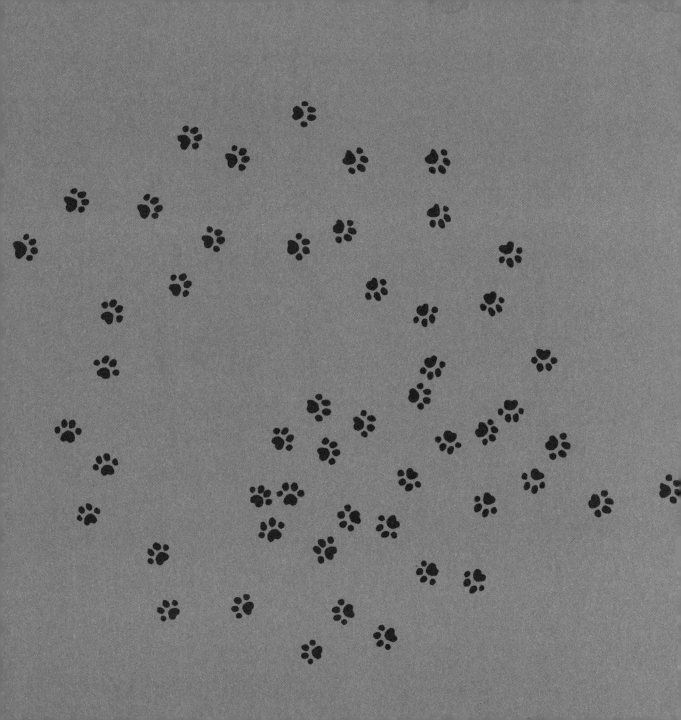